The DNA of Creative Ventures

Ventures

21 Building Blocks of Success

Table of Contents

Introduction

CREATIVE VENTURES

The two most common questions I am asked are:

Do you have a book?

and

How do you guys do what you do?

You would think that by now I would have a book, right? Well, despite being really good at writing articles and newsletters, I am apparently horrible at the discipline of writing a book. I guess it's the left over irresponsibility from my surfing days. The next question revolves around our processes as a strategic consulting firm. For 27 years, we have been providing strategic services to companies ranging from General Mills to Wells Fargo. We have sustained this level of idea development and application by following a set of Laws that govern the way we approach projects. So, due to pressure from a wide variety of sources, I have actually started the process of connecting some ideas in a patterned format.

This eBook introduces the 21 building blocks or laws that make up the foundation of our approaches.

Though there is probably a lot more to each of these, I restricted their explanations to short summaries. I figured that if you are interested enough to acquire this piece, you could dedicate enough time for a quick read on each idea.

So, here you go, an actual shot at answering the two most common questions:

Do you have a book? Kind of. It's an eBook.

How do you guys do what you do? Well, here is our road map - the 21 Building Blocks of Creative Ventures.

Happy reading.

STEPHEN HARVILL

Building Block 1: Speed vs. Thought

Speed should never outweigh thought. Nothing, and I mean nothing, condemns an idea faster than speed. In a world that  *moves at the pace of thunderstorm lightning, we often feel compelled to match the insanity of faster and faster.*

I have seen the impact of speed over thought from every perspective imaginable, including the disasters I have brought upon myself by not taking   the right amount of time to THINK. Just like Maverick and Goose in Top Gun (yes, that is one of many movie references that weave their way through my stuff), we all "feel the need for speed."

When you are working on a project, there is inevitably a timeline, a schedule, a deadline (do you know why they call it a deadline???). It takes a real sense of discipline to SLOW DOWN, but it is a critical element in the success of any project.

I am often involved in strategic meetings where a client is trying –and I mean TRYING– to explain the problem, need or even a solution idea that is so jumbled in confusion and disconnected thought that I have to put up my hand and say, "Slow down!" I will then ask, "Honestly, does *anyone really understand what is going on?" If the meeting were a cartoon, everyone would have a question mark over his or her head.*

There are classic symptoms of speed damage:

- *The project seems to be out of control.*
- *Nobody really knows what's going on.*
- *The final impact is lost in the process.*

Speed buries clarity. Speed shoots ideas off course. Speed makes smart people sound crazy. "Talking to you is like playing bagpipes in an ukulele band!"

This concept, Speed should never outweigh

thought, *is meant to help you take advantage of what you know. It is specifically created to help you leverage experience and find opportunity that is often missed when operating at light speed.*

Slow down a little and discover how incredibly smart you are!

Building Block 2: The Last Cab Leaving

Energy is a tangible thing. You can "feel" the impact of gravity. You can see a light bulb shatter the darkness. You know that your car moves based on energy. These are all great examples of the kind of

energy that immediately impacts our brains by having a

distinct physical effect. But there are other forms of energy as real as the power that sends your plane from Dallas to Hawaii, but eludes your direct   impact.

Emotional momentum is one of those kinds of energy. You have most likely watched a sporting event where a team catches fire and they just can't miss. Time and time again, they seem to do unbelievable things in a short period of time. The opposing team calls a timeout in an effort to thwart their momentum. Now you can't measure that kind of energy in any standard format. There are no joules, no kilowatts, and no calories, but momentum is as real as any of those.

Both good and bad meetings create momentum. Bad experiences are etched in our memory and draw us away from wanting to repeat the experience and require recovery by those in charge of the meeting. Great meetings create their own energy fields and these very real forms of human vitality need to be leveraged for their maximum impact.

Often, companies pat themselves on the back after the "last cab leaves", congratulating each other on a job well done then they head back to work. WRONG!

The momentum of a great experience needs to be recaptured so that participants can continue the positive energy they created and accumulated. Companies need strong, unique, and impactful follow-up strategies so they can take strategic advantage of the energy they created.

Don't let the last cab leaving END the experience; instead, become a Jedi Energy

Master and extend the positive experience beyond the classic final act!

Building Block 3: The Rule of Three

We spend a tremendous amount of our consulting time around the idea of SIMPLE. Simplicity is one of the great business movements dominating strategic planning activities. Customers want SIMPLE.

Though simplicity has been a core tenet of Creative Ventures since its inception, it remains a very difficult goal. The first reason is that people confuse simple with easy. Easy means a lack of effort and simple means a lack of complexity. Getting to simple is NOT EASY!

The second roadblock is that simple

requires "strategic discipline". You have to drive simplicity as a core cultural belief.

If you have a firm understanding of these to barriers, simple IS within your strategic grasp.

We follow a formula and we are doggedly determined in our pursuit of its application. We call it The Rule of Three. In the simplest of terms, no solution, process, or systemic approach to an issue or problem can exceed three parts. PERIOD.

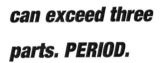

How do you take something that by its very nature is complex? How do you get for example, a sales process, to three if *it's originally a 10-part process? It is called "thoughtful reduction," the ability to bring THINKING to reducing something big to something smaller.*

Here is an example. Most TV remote controls have +/- 47 buttons. Yet, the average user only pushes 7. So if YOU were to redesign a remote control for your TV, how would you make it simple? When teaching simplicity to companies, this is an actual exercise. To make it simpler, you would think about each button and remove some or change their access to achieve a better remote control. THOUGHTFUL REDUCTION. This process is the key to THE RULE OF THREE. The brain can handle three. The average juggler can do three balls, but only 3 out of 100 can juggle 4 balls.

Simple is a formidable goal but with strategic discipline, it can shift the very axis of your business!

Building Block 4: Cause and Effect

We are a business community of firefighters. We scurry from fire to fire, extinguishing problems. A flare-up occurs and we see it  *as another fire. The reality is that we are constantly dealing with recurring problems. Some are easily identified. Others are disguised as something new, but as we pour the water of our time and intellectual resources on it, we begin to come to a slow realization... we have seen it before.*

We are victims of "effect". We are driven to it like a moth to light. We think if we could just fix it, we could move on to something that would create real value. This fixation on the regular problems of our business life is actually a comfortable place. It is built around what we have always been told: there's a problem, solve it, and solve it quickly. Heck, create a system or a process that, in theory, will either stop the problem from happening again or deal with the aftermath.

What if you simply slowed down and took a very critical look at this fire and thought, "What the hell caused this fire?" Yes, I might have to put it out BUT if I knew where the point of ignition was, perhaps I could prevent the fire not only from flaring *up, but also from rekindling!*

I am often asked to take a look at systems and processes that either no longer do what they are supposed to or that have developed bottlenecks, usually through becoming more and more complex, growing bigger and bigger. The key starting point to developing an understanding, no matter if the business is financial services or the fast food industry, is to examine the space that exists between cause and effect. That space is filled with information.

Recently, a client asked me if I could help redesign their client experience because they were struggling with the fact that the benefit of their service was always separated by time. These gaps of time were roadblocks to engaging clients in their model. My attack point was the incredible leverage that existed in the space between cause and effect. Within a couple of hours, we had drafted the design of a plan that ONLY focused on the space they thought was a problem.

The space between cause and effect is the critical point of understanding. By leveraging its appreciation, you find a new way to create impact.

Building Block 5: The Rule of Seeing

I know, I know. You have all heard that "the eyes are the window to the soul." Well, I'll be damned... IT'S TRUE.

The quickest way to discover a solution to a problem, to the development of an idea, to the uncovering of opportunity, is to SEE it.

The brain has basically five highways to garnering data and information. Yep, the five senses. Each plays a vital role in building our physical understanding of the world, hearing and

seeing being the big impact players. Though hearing plays at about 7.5%, it is through seeing that we build our hard drives. Seeing is estimated to make up 87% of all the information we have ever taken in during our lives. In fact, our understanding of light and dark starts in our pre-birth liquid home.

Our visual language opens the portal of creative thinking and helps to us to understand abstract thoughts and high information density.

I have an entire wall in my office covered with auto glass that is turned it into a huge sketchpad. I begin every project at this empty glass wall that is just waiting for an idea to take form.

Walt Disney knew this when he created the idea of storyboarding or sketching out what the connected ideas of a movie might "look" like.

Here is the RULE: if you don't see it, you probably don't get it. PERIOD.

So learn to sketch. Write things out. Invite more eyes. Set up more face-to-face interactions. Get out and "see" your clients. Draw an idea and watch the traditional huge question mark that usually appears overhead vanish.

We are creatures of the light, open your eyes, and invite in a picture.

Building Block 6: The Same Wind Blows

Competitive niches share startling similarities. If you are fighting for business in what you think is the unique market of insurance, guess what? So are your competitors. The niche of market opportunities is the same. Each of you is fighting for company share, of buying opportunities as well as the ups and downs of economic shifts. Strangely enough, "the same wind blows" for everyone.

In 1470, a young explorer from the tiny

country of Portugal set sail into the unknown with the goal of sailing around the world, a world that most believed to be flat. Magellan had the same type of boats that the powers of Europe had, the same boats that England, France, Italy and Spain had sitting in their ports. The same wind was blowing for each and every one of them. The difference? Well, the difference was that Magellan set his sails. He pointed them strategically into a wind that, for all he knew, was sending him to an abyss as dark as a moonless night.

This idea of setting your sails in a unique and impactful direction is one of the keys in succeeding in difficult times.

Ever wonder how a company seems to rise to a different level in what is clearly a crowded and homogenized market? A company decides to do something new, something full of risk, but not unheard of. How did luggage come to have wheels? You know that ever since the first trunk was packed that someone said, "Damn, this is heavy." Why did it take so long to get duct tape in a color other than silver? Why did the most popular cereal in the world, Cheerios, decide to add a flavor to what was already a market-dominant brand? For all their competitors the same wind was blowing, but 3M, General Mills, and U.S. Luggage pointed their sails in a different direction.

Where is your wind blowing? When I get stale, I look to the wind and I'm encouraged to try a new idea, work a new *strategy or look for a new niche to give me that* Magellan *advantage.*

I know it's the same wind for everyone; it's only a matter of how you set your sails.

Building Block 7: Presence

When working with young people, I am always amazed that they are given the advice of "Just showing up is half the battle" or that "Just showing up is often enough." *This makes me want to scream!*

In a world where each every one of is fighting a to create  *and us war*

value, presence is NOT enough.

During a recent site visit to a client that has a huge company and employs over 1,000 people in just one of their offices, I was walking one of the floors that were abuzz with activity. Cubicles were active as far as the eye could see. I asked my host, "What are all these people doing?" His answer was, "I have no idea." Not surprising. There was no way he could know. He did answer, "This floor is account management." I asked if I could jump into one of the small conference rooms and visit with a couple of these folks and he said, "Sure, that's kind of what you're here for."

I asked a bright young woman what she did. She gave me a detailed explanation and I asked her, "Are you making a difference in this company?" She didn't blink at the question and said, "If I wasn't, I wouldn't be here."

Presence wasn't enough for her; she knew her work made a difference.

Every report I write has a unique graphic look. Every presentation I do has specific style and feel. I rehearse my stage presentations dozens of times before I get on a plane. I NEVER just show up. Forget about just being there. The famous author and theologian Rabbi Harold Kushner says, "At the end of the day, what matters is making a difference."

Building Block 8: The Architecture of Time

Most people have the wrong idea about time. I can't really blame them; it's been learned through years of scholastic indoctrination. They think of time as linear. They did time lines about the 100-Year War. They draw lines through consecutive meeting days on their calendars. Time to them is a line, restrictive and rigid. They HAVE to be here or there.

They have missed the boat on this one.

Time is anything but a line. It is anything but firm and unforgiving. Time is more like a rubber band that can bend and shift to anything you think and desire.

It's true.

Ask a crowd to raise their hand if they wished they had more time to read, garden, go to the movies, learn how to cook or any myriad of activities and almost all of them will raise their hands. Amazing. The reality is they ALL have the time to do any of these activities, but they have chosen to do something else.

Time is about choice. You and, believe it or not, no one else but you gets to choose how you invest this most valuable resource.

If you want to exercise, CHOOSE to spend time exercising. Sure, this means that something else loses that time frame, but that's a choice.

If someone tells me they didn't have time to finish a project (something I usually only hear once), I simply ask "What did you do instead?"

To become a more powerful person, learn to choose the use of your time wisely. Learn to discover priorities and impact in your time decision process.

You won't be right all the time, but even Einstein decided to take a walk on the beach every once in a while, leaving the mysteries of the universe to another time!

Building Block 9: The Rule of Everything

When Albert Einstein lay on his death bed, he was still desperately trying to find a  *formula for* **the** Theory **of** **Everything,** *a universal* **equation** *that would*

that would tie together the behavior of the physical world on both the macro and micro level. In the end, everything eluded him.

We often believe that the more we do, the

more valuable we will be. We create these death spirals of spinning tasks and priorities. These can happen both by intention and by lack of paying attention.

First, by intention: when someone starts a position, they determine their value proposition or what they can do that makes them the most valuable person to their company. They figure "The more I can do the better (see The Rule of Abundance)", but the more they do the less focus they have. The next thing you know, they are doing a ton of stuff and doing each of them poorly. Everything is not the answer. Focus is.

When I started Creative Ventures, I did everything from Viking Funerals to screen door repair. I soon discovered that's not a *value statement. I refined the focus to Presentation, Education, and Application (consulting) and watched my little venture grow.*

You have to pay attention. Systems grow by their very nature and if not monitored, they can rapidly become a black hole, sucking in activities that in no way were ever intended. Soon, the system tries to do everything and the initial design is lost due to a lack of attention. Systems are great tools for recurring issues IF they are monitored. If not, the system will destroy its intended purpose (think of phone trees).

Stop searching for the next thing you can add to your perceived value and refine your focus to impact.

When you do everything, you do nothing!

Building Block 10: Paint it Red

Years ago, I was working on a real estate project in Colorado. It was a big deal and I was just a kid at the time. The project was a master-planned community and was loaded with a voluminous book of rules

and regulations that governed everything, from housing types and sizes to where you could and could not park vehicles. I was sure that to be accepted, all of my contributions and ideas had to fit these restrictive parameters and I learned to walk the narrow corridors those rules created.

During one meeting early in the development process, I was presenting ideas around the design of a major recreation facility that would provide swimming, tennis, meeting space, and even a restaurant. One of the founders of the development company asked if the building could be painted "umber". I was kind of startled by the question, mainly because I had no idea what the color *"umber" was. I answered in a quickstep mental dance that there was a pallet of colors approved by the city that we had to work within and was lucky enough to have it with me. I presented it and he said there was no "umber" in the pallet, but he wanted the building to be "umber". About a month later, the next meeting of the development company was held and he point blank asked me why the building wasn't umber (a shade of red) and I again explained it was not an approved color.*

A wonderful man who would later become one of my mentors pulled me aside after the meeting and asked if I was morally opposed to the color? I said, "No, it just didn't fit the tiny color range squeezed into the rules." He told me, "Steve, sometimes you just have to paint the damn thing RED!"

Rules and guidelines play critical roles in the success of projects BUT you have to learn what is and isn't important in the scope of a desired outcome. I was fighting for something that matter little in the greater picture.

Learn what is and isn't important and realize that at times, you just have to PAINT IT RED and move on.

Building Block 11: Outside the Frame

We live, work, think, and believe within the framework we have created. This framework is both a good and a bad thing. First, we can relate our success to this structure. Our knowledge and life experience applied to what we do further strengthens the frame we built until we believe that everything and anything that

*matters is contained within this enclosed world. We bypass everything that's going on outside*

our frame. *"It can't be that important."* How can it impact me?

We have all discovered how big the impact can be from outside the frame. Who'd have thought that a small country like Greece could so impact the global economy? Or that a shift in interest rates can impact everything my clients are doing? Or the simple confidence that it's OK to spend a little money when things are so chaotic? Stuff outside the frame is damn influential!

The building block *"Outside the Frame"* says open your eyes and ears to opportunities happening just outside of your focus. Industries totally unrelated to yours are developing ideas, systems, and processes that can have a huge POSITIVE impact on those   paying attention.

Expand YOU!

Here is just one example: marketing is an almost universal business activity. Take a look at the marketing ideas being used in successful companies irrespective of the industry. What can you learn, what can you copy, what part of their success can be rearranged to meet your needs? What can you learn and apply to your FRAME? Subscribe to advertising publications; find websites that highlight word-of-mouth marketing plans. Move on to how businesses generate referrals. Can the strong referral system in a dental practice teach you how to generate referrals in the financial services business? YES!

Work hard in your framework, but spend valuable time peeking outside and find out

what the world can teach you.

Building Block 12: Never Ask a Fish About Water

Do you ever look at a goldfish hanging out in a fishbowl and wonder, "What the heck is that fish thinking about?" It has a singular existence. It occupies a world of tepid water and limited views. Yet, it is the only world it knows. If you were to ask, "Hey, how's the water?" You would get the

answer *"What's water?"*

Companies often find themselves in goldfish land. It's a world of singularity, just like the goldfish's view. Everything is viewed only through a lens of insurance, financial services, food and beverage, medical, technology, and so on. The bigger world is just passing you by.

Now, don't get me wrong. You need a strong and expansive understanding of what you do, who you serve, and where your business is going, but it doesn't have to be at the exclusion of the greater world.

During a recent offering of THE IDEA FACTORY workshop that featured participants from a single industry, we tested our NEVER ASK A FISH ABOUT THE

WATER idea. In small groups, I asked them to list three game-changing ideas that were currently "in play" and making a difference in ANY industry OUTSIDE of financial services. Guess what? They struggled. They had a hard time thinking about things outside their fishbowl.

3M spends strategic time doing nothing but looking at ideas – from EVERYWHERE. Dr. Buckminster Fuller developed the geodesic dome from looking at an insect's eye. The annual 4C Conference brings together leaders in the cattle industry for the single purpose of viewing ideas and solutions from other industries. The event has a wait list.

Bring your vision up, get out of your fishbowl, and take a look at what the hell everyone else is doing. You will discover new ideas that will bring you leverage and impact!

Building Block 13: Weight

I am sure you have all seen a depiction of Lady Justice holding a set of scales and a double-edged sword. The scales depict the weight of truth and one side is heavier than the other. This represents the shift of the weight of truth as each side argues for their position. The idea of weight, of something being more

important than something else is a critical way of thinking when approaching leadership.

All processes, systems, and decisions carry weight. This weight represents levels of importance. Good leaders understand that within a system, nothing is ever equal. Nothing ever perfectly balances and in fact, perfect balance is NOT the goal.

The search for balance is the modern day equivalent of looking for a unicorn. Balance is a foolish goal to begin with. Have you ever seen a balanced system, a system of equilibrium? When a system achieves balance, the energy moves towards a minimum value and actually reaches zero, at perfect balance. So a balanced system has zero energy. That's not what you are looking for. You want a system or process to be full of energy and, at the same time, be able to know which part of that system deserves your energy or where the weight of the system is.

By understanding that all systems have key elements that need more attention than others, you begin to lead.

For example, in a customer service system, the point of personal contact contains a larger weight than other parts.

Leaders understand that systems and processes have a certain weight. They focus their leadership attention on the elements that produce the highest results. They focus on WEIGHT!

Building Block 14: The One-Time Spark

Ideas are powerful things! When presented properly, a new idea can turn our heads, can make us sit upright, and turn on our active listening. A bright idea can make us put aside what we are doing and get ready to embark upon a pathway lighted anew by this bright and shining revelation. Ideas are dangerous like that. They often ignite the one-time activity and the one-time activity usually causes disasters.

I cannot tell you how many times I have seen "the one-time spark" lead to disappointment fueled by limited excitement.

Here is what I mean. I worked with a client on a unique design for the biannual meeting. They were thrilled about a new way to approach their meetings that had devolved into a repetitive and mundane event. The new meeting was filled with interaction, strong visual presentations, and connections with the participants that extended the meeting way past its conclusion (see The Law of the Last Cab Leaving). The meeting was a huge success. I warned them that going back to the old meeting format was not an option. They now had a new way of creating "meeting value". Alas, the next meeting, they went to their default design and the entire hotel was filled with disappointment. That was the horrible impact of a ONE-TIME SPARK.

The power of a spark that ignites an idea is in its sustainability. Energy needs to be focused on keeping the spark burning or better yet, allow the spark to ignite another idea until you have sparks everywhere.

The one-time shot at making impact is more disastrous than doing nothing.

Connect your sparks and discover what true idea impact means!

Building Block 15: The Delighted End User

Focus is a real issue in the development of strategic platforms. Where do you look to leverage the system? Where can you make the most impact? These are the daily issues we deal with when looking to create value around a client's project. It is particularly true when there are multiple parties involved in the strategy.

Sometimes its best to have a defined starting point, a place to focus both your ideas and your energy. We like to start with the "end user". Who is the final benefactor of this idea?

A couple of years, ago we were hired to work with an advertising agency charged with helping a client launch a  digital music site that would be part of their new corporate strategy. After a series of meetings, the focus of the work became blurred. This is not uncommon when there are multiple parties involved in the project. There was the client looking to enter the digital music space. There was the advertising agency, and there was us. Oh, there was also the buyer of this digital music - the END USER.

Enter THE DELIGHTED END USER. We rapidly eliminated the actual client from the strategy and began our focus on the "end user" - that person we are looking at tear away from a couple of other digital music sites to buy from this client. We focused our strategy on them.

Here is how it works. IF the ultimate end user is delighted, then EVERYONE is delighted. This focus gave us the latitude to think beyond the client's specific needs and creatively plan for the music buyer.

We didn't knock iTunes off their feet, but we created impact!

Building Block 16: Don't Waste Good

Whoa, slow down before you hit that "Delete" key;  *there might be some leverage you are missing. I am shocked at how fast people pass over a success and move on to the next project. "Yeah, we won", "Yes sir, we hit our sales goals" or perhaps, "Now we can finally catch our breath". The next thing you know is that the hidden opportunity that lies in every victory is missed. Poof, it's gone.*

I often fell into this crack early in my

career. *The next idea, the next bright and shiny toy would jazz me. But as my consulting practice grew, I learned to leverage our building block of SPEED SHOULD NEVER OUTWEIGH THOUGHT.*

After each success, I would spend time taking apart the idea. I would look for ways to leverage the success that, based on the existing momentum, would give me LEVERAGE. By leverage, I mean something that would have minimum effort and garner a maximum return.

Most companies don't think leverage.

Here is an example: I launch a new strategy for a client that gets an almost immediate enrollment from those who will participate and be impacted. I realize that this strategy has compatible impact to other divisions of the company. Based on the success of the launch, I discover a simple customization that makes it fit two other divisions. I didn't waste the GOOD. In the past, I would have missed that opportunity by basking in the glow of the success.

Good has a ton of potential when given strong critical examination.

Slow down and take a look at your "good stuff"; it has legs.

Building Block 17: Creative Restriction

Everyone is always looking for creative freedom. Do I have creative freedom to do this or that? We dream of unrestricted access to the idea-creation machine and all the wonderful things we could do with unlimited resources, all the time we need **and**

wide

open

spaces. BUT on the way to all that independence, we soon discover it is really hard to limit our choices to a single direction. Our idea begins to look like the toothpaste aisle at the supermarket where there are 80 tubes to choose from.

The reality is that restrictions actually enhance the creative process. It's true!

When given a smaller space to work an idea, we challenge our creative process and we push the barriers that appear to limit us.

When Walt Disney built Disneyland, he surrounded the theme park with a magnificent railroad that would move guests around the park. Walt loved trains. But the railroad created a restrictive border limiting the expansion of the park. When faced with this constraint, the Imagineers developed an underground approach to *rides. In the Haunted Mansion the expanding room (one of the favorite features of the ride), is actually an elevator taking you down to the ride. This is creativity brought on by limitations.*

Jack White of the rock band The White Stripes understands the creative power of restrictions and will book a recording studio for only 10 days, challenging his writing, producing and recording talents. Restrictions can enhance the creative process. He also embraces the idea of three. All their CD covers face the artistic restriction of using only three colors.

The next time you are looking for the creative response to a problem, allow the problem to create a restrictive space and challenge your way of thinking to see how expansive a border can really be.

Building Block 18: The Rule of Abundance

Here is simplest explanation of this rule:
MORE IS NOT BETTER AND BETTER IS NOT BEST.

We live in a "more" world. When you try to buy a medium soft drink at the movies, they will upsell you the large for only $0.25 more. "No thanks, medium is fine." "But dude, it's only a QUARTER!" Hey, I did the math kid. I just don't want a hot tub of Dr. Pepper. It's extra large this and you get 10% more that. It hits us so hard that we begin to believe that the greatest value is found in more, but I would challenge that thought. It's NOT!

When our focus becomes diluted, so does our impact.

During a recent strategy session for a client, I asked them to list all the value-added programs they bring to their client base. When we were done, there were 20 programs on the whiteboard. I then asked them to grade the programs on those used most and those that they rate the highest value. Guess what? Yep, they were doing things  they weren't very good at. Get rid of them and focus on the programs you do best.

The added time and energy will drive you to BEST.

The Rule of Abundance is a great strategic filter. When you have a list of things to choose from, simply ask which of these are the BEST and drive your focus on those items. Sure, it takes discipline, but the results will provide your clients with the reason they chose you and not someone else doing the exact same thing.

Daniel Day Lewis may be considered the greatest male actor of all time as he is the only one to win three best actor Oscars. He rarely acts. It had been 5 years between roles before he gave his epic performance as Lincoln. When asked why he makes so

few films compared to other actors he
answered, "I sacrifice abundance for
BEST!"

Building Block 19: Fair vs. Equal

I think this law first began to develop when I was a kid sneaking into the UCLA basketball practices to watch and listen to one of the great heroes in my life, John Wooden. I remember reading the great book They Call Me Coach *and understanding his comments on equal versus fair. He said to treat each player equally was unfair to the player. Everyone responds differently. Some require encouragement and some require challenge. He said, "I work towards fair, never equal."*

Fair is the goal. It requires common sense, flexibility, and good judgment. It involves you knowing what's going on, determining fact from fiction, and knowing the players.

Equal is a default and requires little, if any, leadership. Besides, you don't really want it anyway.

Would you want a doctor that treats every headache the same, despite one being caused by allergies and one being caused by a tumor?

In the documentary <u>The History of the Eagles</u>, *one of the epic fights (and there were many) within the rock band was around pay. Don Henley and Glenn Frey were paid more than other members of the band. They wrote and sang most of the songs. But one band mate wanted everything to be equal, despite making a sizable check from his superb talents. The friction between fair and equal caused an emotional explosion.*

It's time to cut the pie and the two kids are waiting for a piece. The wise mom tells them, one of you can cut the pie and the other gets to choose the first piece. Hmmmm, that's what I mean by fair.

Building Block 20: Structural Support

It is probably no surprise to you that the foundational support of a building is pretty damn important to its structural integrity. Arches, beams, and columns serve a key physical purpose of supporting and resisting loads. What is underground and behind the scenes is critical to success. If

that is taken as a fact, why then does the support structure of a company almost always take a backseat to everything else? Why is the focus of training and education centered on leadership, management, and sales? Why is the support of the core aspects of the company not a critical strategic element of a company's planning?

It is because of our arrogant approach to what we believe are routine tasks. Structural support is NOT about making copies and filing. It IS about making sure every aspect, from sales to profit margins, is goal-bound.

During a recent planning session for a client, we focused on the skill sets needed in the support services ranks. The list was extensive, good thinkers, quick and versatile, good communicators (both spoken and written), broad base of company and industry knowledge, and friendly made the list. Yet, when we connected these skill sets to training, there was a HUGE void. So, we designed a new approach to enhancing the skill sets of the support staff. During the first communications class, I had a number of people ask me, "What's going on?" "What do you mean," I responded. "Well, we've never had anything like this before." The result was an overwhelming new approach by the support teams to engage in a strategic, connected plan to get better.

A recent study at Howard University of 575 companies quantified this building block. An investment of $680 per employee in training yielded a minimum of a 6% return in shareholder value. How was this investment recognized in performance?

Increase in sales, increase in referrals, increase in retention, increase in new ideas, and an increase in overall customer satisfaction.

Foundations are important; don't ignore their strategic value.

Building Block 21: The Legs Feed the Wolf

This Law was originally The Law of Doing What You Do Best, but after seeing the 2004 movie Miracle *based on the 1980 U. S. Olympic hockey team's win over Russia, I changed it to this. It's more mysterious and poetic. It also sounds way better when you say it.* "The legs feed the wolf" *" was a saying Kurt Russell used when playing coach Herb Brooks. It meant that our conditioning would allow us to win. To me, it meant that you have to know what factors have the greatest impact on success and focus your intensity and vision in those specific areas.*

Brooks knew that if his team was in the best condition, if they could go hard when the other teams were ready to quit, that he could snatch wins out of what looked like defeats.

*The Legs Feed The Wolf is critical to our successful strategic approach with our clients. We always begin our focus on what they do well. Here is the "*legs feed the wolf" *way of thinking: manage your weaknesses but focus time and resources on your strengths. Kind of a backwards*

way of thinking, right? If your child
brought home a report card with A's in
science and math, but a D in geography
and an F in English, you would immediately
focus on the D and F. "How can you get an
F in English? It's your NATIVE language."
The Legs Feed the Wolf *strategy would say,*
"You need to manage the D and F up to
passable grades, but your child's Legs *are*
math and science." The strategy would
work to make your child a math and
science SUPERSTAR!

Knowing what you are truly good at is an
often-undervalued way of thinking. We
spend so much time responding to
perceived market needs, of rushing to the
next product or niche opportunity that we
forget what got us to where we are.

Build on your strengths and manage your weaknesses.

Conclusion

Over the last 27 years, our ideas have been tested in the real world by our clients. In our efforts, we have developed a personal roadmap to success. These building blocks have been refined and condensed over the years to offer insights on our most simplistic, elegant, and powerful methods. We believe that these can be translated to any business and, when introduced into a current system, will prove to be extremely impactful in moving your business forward. Perhaps this information has proved valuable to you, or maybe it was just an interesting read, but moving on from here, there is only one question. What will you DO with it?

About

Creative Ventures is an independent strategic consulting company with its headquarters in Austin, Texas and offices in Dallas, Texas.

We have worked on the development of original ideas in the form of strategic platforms for over 27 years and have had the honor of working with client/partners like PepsiCo, Frito Lay, IBM, General Mills, Wells Fargo, Apple, Allianz, and National Life to name a few.

We do our work in three key areas:

PRESENTATIONS: *Our ideas are delivered in large stage   presentations as* *well as small focused groups. We utilize a multimedia, interactive format.*

EDUCATION: *We teach our core principles as part of companies' training curriculums and have the honor of re-developing core learning strategies, resulting in the development of internal learning universities.*

APPLICATION: *This is our consulting side of the business where we apply our strategic platforms internally for companies.*

You can learn more about our unique and dynamic company by contacting us:

Creativeventures.com

Steve@creativeventures.com

Colin@creativeventures.com

Made in the USA
Middletown, DE
09 February 2015